RECIPE JOURNAL BLANK BOOK SAVE YOUR SPECIAL RECIPES

RECIPE OF THE DAY

INGREDIENTS NEEDED	PREPARATIONS

COOKING DIRECTIONS

NOTES

RECIPE OF THE DAY

INGREDIENTS NEEDED	PREPARATIONS

COOKING DIRECTIONS

NOTES

RECIPE OF THE DAY

INGREDIENTS NEEDED	PREPARATIONS

COOKING DIRECTIONS

NOTES

RECIPE OF THE DAY

INGREDIENTS NEEDED	PREPARATIONS

COOKING DIRECTIONS

NOTES

RECIPE OF THE DAY

INGREDIENTS NEEDED	PREPARATIONS

COOKING DIRECTIONS

NOTES

RECIPE OF THE DAY

INGREDIENTS NEEDED	PREPARATIONS

COOKING DIRECTIONS

NOTES

RECIPE OF THE DAY

INGREDIENTS NEEDED	PREPARATIONS

COOKING DIRECTIONS

NOTES

RECIPE OF THE DAY

INGREDIENTS NEEDED	PREPARATIONS

COOKING DIRECTIONS

NOTES

RECIPE OF THE DAY

INGREDIENTS NEEDED	PREPARATIONS

COOKING DIRECTIONS

NOTES

RECIPE OF THE DAY

INGREDIENTS NEEDED	PREPARATIONS

COOKING DIRECTIONS

NOTES

RECIPE OF THE DAY

INGREDIENTS NEEDED	PREPARATIONS

COOKING DIRECTIONS

NOTES

RECIPE OF THE DAY

INGREDIENTS NEEDED	PREPARATIONS

COOKING DIRECTIONS

NOTES

RECIPE OF THE DAY

INGREDIENTS NEEDED	PREPARATIONS

COOKING DIRECTIONS

NOTES

RECIPE OF THE DAY

INGREDIENTS NEEDED	PREPARATIONS

COOKING DIRECTIONS

NOTES

RECIPE OF THE DAY

INGREDIENTS NEEDED	PREPARATIONS

COOKING DIRECTIONS

NOTES

RECIPE OF THE DAY

INGREDIENTS NEEDED	PREPARATIONS

COOKING DIRECTIONS

NOTES

RECIPE OF THE DAY

INGREDIENTS NEEDED	PREPARATIONS

COOKING DIRECTIONS

NOTES

RECIPE OF THE DAY

INGREDIENTS NEEDED	PREPARATIONS

COOKING DIRECTIONS

NOTES

RECIPE OF THE DAY

INGREDIENTS NEEDED	PREPARATIONS

COOKING DIRECTIONS

NOTES

RECIPE OF THE DAY

INGREDIENTS NEEDED	PREPARATIONS

COOKING DIRECTIONS

NOTES

RECIPE OF THE DAY

INGREDIENTS NEEDED	PREPARATIONS

COOKING DIRECTIONS

NOTES

RECIPE OF THE DAY

INGREDIENTS NEEDED	PREPARATIONS

COOKING DIRECTIONS

NOTES

RECIPE OF THE DAY

INGREDIENTS NEEDED	PREPARATIONS

COOKING DIRECTIONS

NOTES

RECIPE OF THE DAY

INGREDIENTS NEEDED	PREPARATIONS

COOKING DIRECTIONS

NOTES

RECIPE OF THE DAY

INGREDIENTS NEEDED	PREPARATIONS

COOKING DIRECTIONS

NOTES

RECIPE OF THE DAY

INGREDIENTS NEEDED	PREPARATIONS

COOKING DIRECTIONS

NOTES

RECIPE OF THE DAY

INGREDIENTS NEEDED	PREPARATIONS

COOKING DIRECTIONS

NOTES

RECIPE OF THE DAY

INGREDIENTS NEEDED	PREPARATIONS

COOKING DIRECTIONS

NOTES

RECIPE OF THE DAY

INGREDIENTS NEEDED	PREPARATIONS

COOKING DIRECTIONS

NOTES

RECIPE OF THE DAY

INGREDIENTS NEEDED	PREPARATIONS

COOKING DIRECTIONS

NOTES

RECIPE OF THE DAY

INGREDIENTS NEEDED	PREPARATIONS

COOKING DIRECTIONS

NOTES

RECIPE OF THE DAY

INGREDIENTS NEEDED	PREPARATIONS

COOKING DIRECTIONS

NOTES

RECIPE OF THE DAY

INGREDIENTS NEEDED	PREPARATIONS

COOKING DIRECTIONS

NOTES

RECIPE OF THE DAY

INGREDIENTS NEEDED	PREPARATIONS

COOKING DIRECTIONS

NOTES

RECIPE OF THE DAY

INGREDIENTS NEEDED	PREPARATIONS

COOKING DIRECTIONS

NOTES

RECIPE OF THE DAY

INGREDIENTS NEEDED	PREPARATIONS

COOKING DIRECTIONS

NOTES

RECIPE OF THE DAY

INGREDIENTS NEEDED	PREPARATIONS

COOKING DIRECTIONS

NOTES

RECIPE OF THE DAY

INGREDIENTS NEEDED	PREPARATIONS

COOKING DIRECTIONS

NOTES

RECIPE OF THE DAY

INGREDIENTS NEEDED	PREPARATIONS

COOKING DIRECTIONS

NOTES

RECIPE OF THE DAY

INGREDIENTS NEEDED	PREPARATIONS

COOKING DIRECTIONS

NOTES

RECIPE OF THE DAY

INGREDIENTS NEEDED	PREPARATIONS

COOKING DIRECTIONS

NOTES

RECIPE OF THE DAY

INGREDIENTS NEEDED	PREPARATIONS

COOKING DIRECTIONS

NOTES

RECIPE OF THE DAY

INGREDIENTS NEEDED	PREPARATIONS

COOKING DIRECTIONS

NOTES

RECIPE OF THE DAY

INGREDIENTS NEEDED	PREPARATIONS

COOKING DIRECTIONS

NOTES

RECIPE OF THE DAY

INGREDIENTS NEEDED	PREPARATIONS

COOKING DIRECTIONS

NOTES

RECIPE OF THE DAY

INGREDIENTS NEEDED	PREPARATIONS

COOKING DIRECTIONS

NOTES

RECIPE OF THE DAY

INGREDIENTS NEEDED	PREPARATIONS

COOKING DIRECTIONS

NOTES

RECIPE OF THE DAY

INGREDIENTS NEEDED	PREPARATIONS

COOKING DIRECTIONS

NOTES

RECIPE OF THE DAY

INGREDIENTS NEEDED	PREPARATIONS

COOKING DIRECTIONS

NOTES

RECIPE OF THE DAY

INGREDIENTS NEEDED	PREPARATIONS

COOKING DIRECTIONS

NOTES

RECIPE OF THE DAY

INGREDIENTS NEEDED	PREPARATIONS

COOKING DIRECTIONS

NOTES

RECIPE OF THE DAY

INGREDIENTS NEEDED	PREPARATIONS

COOKING DIRECTIONS

NOTES

RECIPE OF THE DAY

INGREDIENTS NEEDED	PREPARATIONS

COOKING DIRECTIONS

NOTES

RECIPE OF THE DAY

INGREDIENTS NEEDED	PREPARATIONS

COOKING DIRECTIONS

NOTES

RECIPE OF THE DAY

INGREDIENTS NEEDED	PREPARATIONS

COOKING DIRECTIONS

NOTES

RECIPE OF THE DAY

INGREDIENTS NEEDED	PREPARATIONS

COOKING DIRECTIONS

NOTES

RECIPE OF THE DAY

INGREDIENTS NEEDED	PREPARATIONS

COOKING DIRECTIONS

NOTES

RECIPE OF THE DAY

INGREDIENTS NEEDED	PREPARATIONS

COOKING DIRECTIONS

NOTES

RECIPE OF THE DAY

INGREDIENTS NEEDED	PREPARATIONS

COOKING DIRECTIONS

NOTES

RECIPE OF THE DAY

INGREDIENTS NEEDED	PREPARATIONS

COOKING DIRECTIONS

NOTES

RECIPE OF THE DAY

INGREDIENTS NEEDED	PREPARATIONS

COOKING DIRECTIONS

NOTES

RECIPE OF THE DAY

INGREDIENTS NEEDED	PREPARATIONS

COOKING DIRECTIONS

NOTES

RECIPE OF THE DAY

INGREDIENTS NEEDED	PREPARATIONS

COOKING DIRECTIONS

NOTES

RECIPE OF THE DAY

INGREDIENTS NEEDED	PREPARATIONS

COOKING DIRECTIONS

NOTES

RECIPE OF THE DAY

INGREDIENTS NEEDED	PREPARATIONS

COOKING DIRECTIONS

NOTES

RECIPE OF THE DAY

INGREDIENTS NEEDED	PREPARATIONS

COOKING DIRECTIONS

NOTES

RECIPE OF THE DAY

INGREDIENTS NEEDED	PREPARATIONS

COOKING DIRECTIONS

NOTES

RECIPE OF THE DAY

INGREDIENTS NEEDED	PREPARATIONS

COOKING DIRECTIONS

NOTES

RECIPE OF THE DAY

INGREDIENTS NEEDED	PREPARATIONS

COOKING DIRECTIONS

NOTES

RECIPE OF THE DAY

INGREDIENTS NEEDED	PREPARATIONS

COOKING DIRECTIONS

NOTES

RECIPE OF THE DAY

INGREDIENTS NEEDED	PREPARATIONS

COOKING DIRECTIONS

NOTES

RECIPE OF THE DAY

INGREDIENTS NEEDED	PREPARATIONS

COOKING DIRECTIONS

NOTES

RECIPE OF THE DAY

INGREDIENTS NEEDED	PREPARATIONS

COOKING DIRECTIONS

NOTES

RECIPE OF THE DAY

INGREDIENTS NEEDED	PREPARATIONS

COOKING DIRECTIONS

NOTES

RECIPE OF THE DAY

INGREDIENTS NEEDED	PREPARATIONS

COOKING DIRECTIONS

NOTES

RECIPE OF THE DAY

INGREDIENTS NEEDED	PREPARATIONS

COOKING DIRECTIONS

NOTES

RECIPE OF THE DAY

INGREDIENTS NEEDED	PREPARATIONS

COOKING DIRECTIONS

NOTES

RECIPE OF THE DAY

INGREDIENTS NEEDED	PREPARATIONS

COOKING DIRECTIONS

NOTES

RECIPE OF THE DAY

INGREDIENTS NEEDED	PREPARATIONS

COOKING DIRECTIONS

NOTES

RECIPE OF THE DAY

INGREDIENTS NEEDED	PREPARATIONS

COOKING DIRECTIONS

NOTES

RECIPE OF THE DAY

INGREDIENTS NEEDED	PREPARATIONS

COOKING DIRECTIONS

NOTES

RECIPE OF THE DAY

INGREDIENTS NEEDED	PREPARATIONS

COOKING DIRECTIONS

NOTES

RECIPE OF THE DAY

INGREDIENTS NEEDED	PREPARATIONS

COOKING DIRECTIONS

NOTES

RECIPE OF THE DAY

INGREDIENTS NEEDED	PREPARATIONS

COOKING DIRECTIONS

NOTES

RECIPE OF THE DAY

INGREDIENTS NEEDED	PREPARATIONS

COOKING DIRECTIONS

NOTES

RECIPE OF THE DAY

INGREDIENTS NEEDED	PREPARATIONS

COOKING DIRECTIONS

NOTES

RECIPE OF THE DAY

INGREDIENTS NEEDED	PREPARATIONS

COOKING DIRECTIONS

NOTES

RECIPE OF THE DAY

INGREDIENTS NEEDED	PREPARATIONS

COOKING DIRECTIONS

NOTES

RECIPE OF THE DAY

INGREDIENTS NEEDED	PREPARATIONS

COOKING DIRECTIONS

NOTES

RECIPE OF THE DAY

INGREDIENTS NEEDED	PREPARATIONS

COOKING DIRECTIONS

NOTES

RECIPE OF THE DAY

INGREDIENTS NEEDED	PREPARATIONS

COOKING DIRECTIONS

NOTES

RECIPE OF THE DAY

INGREDIENTS NEEDED	PREPARATIONS

COOKING DIRECTIONS

NOTES

RECIPE OF THE DAY

INGREDIENTS NEEDED	PREPARATIONS

COOKING DIRECTIONS

NOTES

RECIPE OF THE DAY

INGREDIENTS NEEDED	PREPARATIONS

COOKING DIRECTIONS

NOTES

RECIPE OF THE DAY

INGREDIENTS NEEDED	PREPARATIONS

COOKING DIRECTIONS

NOTES

RECIPE OF THE DAY

INGREDIENTS NEEDED	PREPARATIONS

COOKING DIRECTIONS

NOTES

RECIPE OF THE DAY

INGREDIENTS NEEDED	PREPARATIONS

COOKING DIRECTIONS

NOTES

RECIPE OF THE DAY

INGREDIENTS NEEDED	PREPARATIONS

COOKING DIRECTIONS

NOTES

RECIPE OF THE DAY

INGREDIENTS NEEDED	PREPARATIONS

COOKING DIRECTIONS

NOTES

RECIPE OF THE DAY

INGREDIENTS NEEDED	PREPARATIONS

COOKING DIRECTIONS

NOTES

RECIPE OF THE DAY

INGREDIENTS NEEDED	PREPARATIONS

COOKING DIRECTIONS

NOTES

RECIPE OF THE DAY

INGREDIENTS NEEDED	PREPARATIONS

COOKING DIRECTIONS

NOTES

RECIPE OF THE DAY

INGREDIENTS NEEDED	PREPARATIONS

COOKING DIRECTIONS

NOTES

RECIPE OF THE DAY

INGREDIENTS NEEDED	PREPARATIONS

COOKING DIRECTIONS

NOTES

www.ingramcontent.com/pod-product-compliance
Lightning Source LLC
LaVergne TN
LVHW060823170826
845678LV00010B/1889

* 9 7 9 8 8 6 9 4 5 4 9 6 6 *